REDBIRD
THE STORY OF A CARDINAL

written and illustrated by

ROBERT M. McCLUNG

William Morrow & Company New York

The author wishes to thank the Massachusetts Audubon Society, and all of the interested individuals who helped him to locate and observe nesting cardinals, and who generously supplied him with information and material.

Patches of snow still covered most of the ground, but tree buds were swelling in the warm sunshine. Honeybees buzzed around the crocus, and newly arrived robins hopped about looking for earthworms. On this last day of March, spring was in the air.

A nuthatch was eating its breakfast at the bird feeder. Then a chickadee flew in to get its share. A downy woodpecker was hammering at a piece of suet on a nearby tree trunk. These birds had been around all winter.

3

A flash of red swept across the snowy lawn and landed at the feeder, scattering the smaller birds. The newcomer was handsome and bold. He had a bright red coat and a jaunty crest, set off by a black mask and a beard. He was Redbird, the cardinal.

Seizing a sunflower seed in his strong blunt beak, Redbird shelled it expertly and swallowed the kernel. Then another and another went down the same way.

Soon a female cardinal joined him. She was not nearly so brilliant as Redbird. Her color was mostly soft gray-brown, with red trim in her crest and wings and tail.

Redbird shelled a sunflower seed and offered it to his mate. He was paying

more attention to her these days. During the winter he had not allowed her at the feeder until he had eaten all he wanted. But now the season for courtship and nesting was on its way.

The snow soon melted under the warm April sun, and spring came on with a rush. Violets and bloodroot burst into

bloom, and fern fiddleheads poked out of the ground. Bluebirds warbled softly in the meadow, and red-winged black-birds called from the marsh.

Every evening a chorus of spring peepers sounded in the marsh too. And every morning, before dawn, the birds began their chorus of spring song.

Now Redbird began to court his mate in earnest. He followed her about wherever she went and offered her gifts of food. Each morning he flew to a singing post on the topmost branch of a huge elm tree. Raising his crest high, he swelled out his throat and poured forth his clear whistling song over and over.

Whooit — whooit — whooit. Whoit — whoit — whoit, whit — whit — whit, whitwhitwhitwhit. Cheer! Cheer! Cheer!

Sometimes the song sounded like: *Wheat — wheat — wheat, whit — whit — whit. Tchew! Tchew! Tchew!* Redbird was an expert singer and had many calls.

Finished, he would fly to another high perch in a sugar maple tree and repeat his performance. Then on to a dogwood,

9

and across to another big elm. He had a
number of favorite singing posts, which
marked the boundaries of his breeding
territory. His singing warned other male
cardinals to stay away.

Sometimes Redbird's mate joined
in with a song of her own. Her voice
was softer than his, but just as pleasing.
Then off she would fly with Redbird
winging swiftly after her.

When she landed, Redbird would
perch on the limb beside her, his crest
raised and his wings half-spread. There
he swayed slowly back and forth, singing
again, softly this time. He was courting
his mate ardently.

One day in early May, when Redbird was singing from his high perch in the elm tree, another male cardinal answered him. A moment later the strange male burst into view, flying straight toward the tree where the female cardinal sat.

Redbird dove to the attack, and feathers flew as the two males collided in the air. Pausing for breath, they scolded angrily at one another from facing branches. Then Redbird flew at his rival once more.

The chase continued all morning, but at last the other male retreated for good. Redbird flew to his high perch and sang his victory song over and over again.

13

The next day the female cardinal
began to hunt for a good nesting site.
After looking over every tree and shrub
in Redbird's territory, she settled finally
on a bushy hemlock tree. Its dense
branches would shield her nest and help
to hide it.

14

Soon she began to gather nesting material and carry it to the spot she had selected — a branch about six feet from the ground. Redbird kept her company while she worked, but he didn't help to build the nest.

Working only in the mornings, the female cardinal took five days to construct her nest. She made it of slender twigs and weed stems, with a few peelings of bark and dried leaves tucked in. As a final touch, she lined the inside with dried grass. The finished nest was shaped like a shallow bowl about five inches across.

Several days later she laid her first egg. It was greenish-white and had a spattering of brown spots all over it. She laid a second egg the next morning, and her third and last egg the morning after that. Her clutch complete, she began to sit on the three eggs.

While his mate brooded the eggs, Redbird often brought seeds and berries for
her to eat. Sometimes she left the nest
for a few minutes, to eat or drink or
bathe. Then Redbird stayed close to the
eggs and guarded them. He didn't sing
much these days. Singing might give
away the location of the nest to enemies.

One day a female cowbird found the nest, while Redbird's mate was away, and slipped through the branches toward it. Cowbirds often lay their eggs in other birds' nests. These birds then have the job of hatching and raising the young cowbirds. But Redbird flew at the cowbird and drove her away.

19

That same afternoon a chipmunk skittered about on the ground beneath the hemlock. Given the chance, it might climb up the tree and eat the eggs. But not this time. Redbird scolded at the chipmunk, sounding his sharp alarm note, *Tsip! Tsip! Tsip!* He darted down toward the little striped ground squirrel and drove it away too.

Several days later the weather turned suddenly cold and stormy. Rain poured down in torrents, then gradually changed into wet, heavy snow. The hemlock branches drooped low under their white blanket; icicles hung from their tips.

Throughout the storm, the female cardinal sat tight on the nest. If she left the eggs uncovered today, the life within them would soon die. Baby robins in a nearby nest did freeze to death. The unusual May storm ended that evening, however, and the next day the weather was warm and sunny again.

Twelve days after the female cardinal had started to sit on the eggs, a crack appeared in one of them. The baby bird inside was chipping at the shell. The crack became larger, and bits of shell fell away. Redbird's mate could feel the movements beneath her.

Finally the egg broke in two, and a baby cardinal tumbled out. The tiny hatchling was naked and bedraggled, and its eyes were tightly closed. It was so weak and helpless that it could hardly raise its head.

The two remaining eggs hatched the next morning. While his mate brooded the nestlings, Redbird hopped about on the lawn hunting for soft grubs and other insects to feed them.

For the first day or two, Redbird gave the food directly to his mate whenever he returned to the nest. She swallowed the food and partially digested it. Then she pumped it from her own throat into the throats of the babies.

The little cardinals grew very fast. Soft gray down soon covered their bodies, and in several days their eyes began to open. Blue sheaths of flight feathers sprouted on the edges of their wings, and a strip of dark pinfeathers began to grow down each little back.

A week after they had hatched, all three nestlings raised their heads high whenever Redbird or his mate returned to the nest with food. Three yellow-edged beaks gaped as they peeped to be fed.

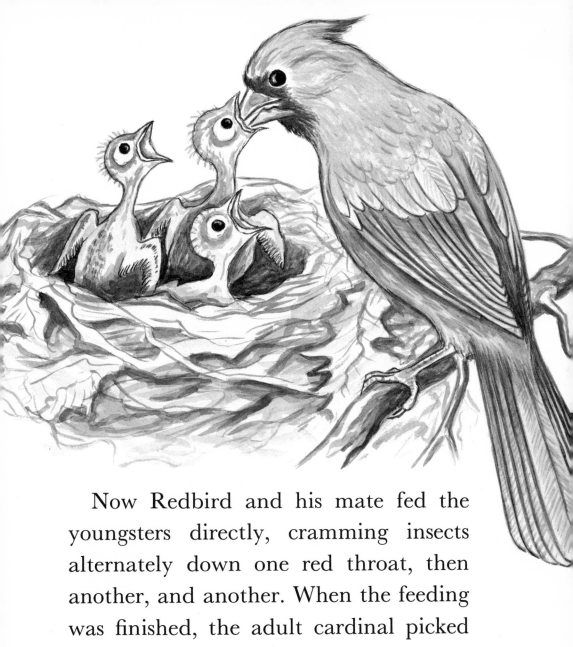

Now Redbird and his mate fed the youngsters directly, cramming insects alternately down one red throat, then another, and another. When the feeding was finished, the adult cardinal picked

up the droppings of the young and carried them away. The nest must be kept clean.

One day a big grackle came to the nest, when both parents were away hunting food. The grackle seized the smallest of the nestlings and flew off with it. Returning, Redbird saw the grackle and gave chase. But he was too late. The young bird was dead when the grackle dropped it.

By the time they were ten days old, the two remaining youngsters had grown so much that they filled the nest. Their skin was almost completely covered by sprouting gray-brown feathers. Caps of wispy down waved from the crown of each little head. The two young cardinals didn't look very much like their parents.

30

Pushing and shoving, they raised themselves on wobbly legs and cheeped greedily for food. They swallowed everything offered with a great deal of blinking and gaping, then begged for more. Satisfied at last, they scratched vigorously under their wings or preened their feathers. Finally they would settle down to sleep.

31

On the twelfth morning after he had hatched, the bigger youngster climbed to the edge of the nest. Teetering to keep his balance, he stretched out to grab a morsel of food from his mother. Suddenly he tumbled off into space. Spreading his wings, he fluttered them frantically. He could fly!

He couldn't steer very well, however, for his tail feathers had hardly sprouted. With a plop he landed under a mountain laurel.

A half hour later the second youngster left the nest too, ending up in the lower branches of a nearby spruce. She started to hop upward from branch to branch.

Both parents hovered anxiously about the young birds, for this was the time of greatest danger. A big spotted cat walked through the yard, on the lookout for whatever he might find. Redbird and his

mate chipped frantically as the cat approached the young bird under the laurel bush. But the cat paid no attention to them. He had spotted the little bird and was making ready to spring.

Redbird swooped down past the cat's head on one side, and his mate swooped past on the other. Confused, the cat drew back and blinked. At that moment the young cardinal took off on uncertain wings and reached a perch in the spruce tree, ten feet above the ground. For the moment he was safe.

A blue jay sailed into the yard, curious to find out what was going on. Redbird and his mate swooped to the attack once more and chased the blue jay out of the yard. Another danger routed.

Day after day Redbird and his mate watched over the fledglings and brought food to them. The youngsters exercised their wings with longer and longer flights, and they preened their growing feathers regularly. A week out of the nest, they were fat and fluffy, twice as big as they had been seven days before. The feathers on their back were dark brown now, while their breast was buffy and mottled.

Ten days afterward the young male was almost as big as his mother. His growing tail was bright red-brown, and he had touches of red in his wings.

Redbird often looked after the young-sters without his mate these days. She was busy building a new nest for a second brood.

By mid-July the young cardinals had been flying for a full month. They had learned how to take dust baths and how to drink at the garden pool. Now no matter how much they begged, Redbird usually refused to feed them. They were able to hunt for insects and seeds and berries for themselves.

When Redbird visited the bird feeder, the two youngsters tagged along and watched while he cracked some sunflower seeds and ate them. The young cardinals quickly began to imitate him. First young Redbird, and then his sister, cracked a seed and ate the kernel.

Soon both Redbird and his mate were busy all the time taking care of their

second brood — four nestlings this time.
The two older youngsters ranged all
over the neighborhood these days, but
their parents often saw them at the bird
feeder or bath.

In late summer young Redbird and his sister moulted, and each grew a new set of feathers. In his red coat young Redbird looked just like his father, while his sister resembled her mother.

Fall arrived, the weather turned crisp and cool, and the leaves changed color. Many birds flew south for the winter, but not the cardinals. They would stay in this area all winter long.

One day, in early November, big soft flakes of snow began to fall. The long cold time had come — but no matter. Redbird flew to the familiar bird feeder and cracked a sunflower seed for himself. Then he flew to his old perch on the elm tree and gave several short whistles.

Cheer! Cheer! Cheer!